# FROM THE GARDEN OF MY SOUL

# FROM THE GARDEN OF MY SOUL

**Selected Poems**

Lorikeet Press, 2024

This is a volume of original poetry.

FROM THE GARDEN OF MY SOUL
SELECTED POEMS
from the 1970s to 2024
written by Alison Handmer

First edition. May 7, 2024.

Copyright © Alison Handmer

ISBN: 978-0-6458483-6-6

All rights reserved. No part of this publication may be reproduced, stored in a retrieval system, or transmitted in any form or by any means, electronic, mechanical, photocopying, recording or otherwise, without the prior permission of the copyright owner and the publisher of this book.

Acknowledgements: *Half Tide Rocks* and *These Trees* first appeared in Central Coast Poetry Society publications.

www.lorikeetpress.com

*For my mother, who helped me shape first words,
and for every member of our family,
and for my cherished friends.*

*Thank you for your patience and encouragement.*

*We share so much of the journey!*

**Contents**

Of new life                     page 9

In suburbia                     page 25

On focus                        page 37

Of love and longing             page 65

On flora and fauna              page 81

On time and place               page 97

Under the moon and sun          page 113

Of grief and gratitude          page 131

# Of new life

## Mask

Why carve with words?
My finger may mark curves
Tracing down a plane of skin
Whose face, upturned
Softly deserves
Some praise it aches to win.

It takes my touch,
Moving, asking,
Letting stain, a shadow, this soft edged mask …

But another brush
Plays on this face.

Blood blush and light create
An image no pen can erase.


1982

## Awaiting birth

Unlock this gate
And let the generations flow
Through me.
Hoping, I wait.
Reward my patience. Go.
Take up your key
Before it's too late
And let the generations flow
Through me.


1987

## Reaching

These are not
the hands of the blind
Shielding from, and reaching for,
Things known.
Like soft breaths on my shoulder,
They touch without intent.
I wonder what demands they'll find
When you and they are grown.
I'll ask you,
When you're older
Just what those gestures meant.


1987 (for Casey)

## Night wonder

Molten,
The sleeping weight of your arm
On mine.
What being is this,
To cuddle and clean
And watch,
I ask,
As he watches,
Cleaned and cuddling,
Wondering what being I am.

1987 (for Casey)

# Brood

You are drinking my yearning
At the lights and laughter
Beyond this hushed, compulsory communion.
Joined, we are excluded — the feeder and the fed —
Held by sweet warm milk
In mutual solitude.
But time, time, my son,
With every swallow
Will turn us out,
Tip us into parties
Where we must be bright.
Then might I glance,
Secretly subdued,
At hushed and darkened rooms,
And brood.

1987

## Babble

Out of the language all once knew
Come your words
Bright coins, you scatter and scatter.
Tell me, as I listen with new ears
Gathering that gold
And warming it,
Heavy with shine.
And even at night
Your bright eyes dark,
Look up to mine
And your voice begins again.

1988

## Future focus

Misty dusk
A milky opal
Is the soft, warm dome of a baby's skull
New and full of future,
The details yet unfocussed.
As distance slowly closes into night

Breath by breath
The baby reaches for definitions.

Clear dawn waits.

The baby wakes.

## To hold

To hold all of you,
Warm child, crying,
Your growing bones
Heavy in my arms…

To hold all of you —
Your hair
So soft at the hollows of my throat
Your body's perfect curves against my own…

To hold all of you,
Comforts us both.


1992 (for Marcus)

# Memory

Memory. Such a beautiful word.
Memories. Dark smooth pebbles
Polished by the tumble of water over time,
Over moments remembered,
Nuggets of past to be found and fondled.
Held in the palm,
before being tossed back,
splashing and sinking in the stream of time.

Remember. Even the pain is washed away,
'til only the meaning remains.
This happened, says the stone.
This was, says the stone.
This moment had meaning,
For the one who holds the stone.

I stand in the stream,
the water cold at my ankles, cold and clear.

Around me, water flows over boulders,
smoothing their curves, soothing, numbing.

A thousand liquid molecules an instant
smash against them, wiping away hard edges.
Tears mean nothing here.

Hear the stream.
It is the sound of time travelling,
of cleansing and remembering,
as I stoop to find a stone.

This was, I say, as the water drips from the stone,
my fingers cold around its weight.
This was how I remember him, my grandfather,
who is gone.

He came to see you, you, so new,
your skin too pink, too big for such small bones.
He held you in his arm,
a wiry arm of 80 years of toil,
his own skin pocked and worn by too much sun
Hands gnarled, the knuckles big
 and barnacled with fixing, making, holding
Holding you, so soft and new.

He held you
and he laughed.


1990 (for Marcus and Hector and Robyn and Richard, and all of us who love the swimming hole at Rozzie's farm in Huonbrook)

# Against the aging

Against the aging
I see you now,
Stooped over your stove
Your reluctant glance
Turned to the unwanted cameraman
Who caught you thus,
Tired at the labour of the day.

I know you loved your other image —
Young and strong and poised
Dressed in your best
And ready for the word

Oh Annie, who I never met —
How you must have longed to share your baby daughters
With the women you left behind.
All those letters
Could never replace the whisper of warmth,
Velvet skin,
So soft against the aging.

And now I grieve that my own new daughter
Cannot be held by yours,
My grandmother,
So old and far away

I stoop and cry.

Tell me, Annie
That we hold each other, always,
All of us,
Reaching down the centuries

Forever tired
Forever beautiful
Soft against the aging.



1994 (for my great grandmother Annie, and my daughter, Annie)

## Daisy astronomy

The daisies outside your window
sweet stars
dancing in the Southerly —
Are the flowers I sewed
on your baby blanket
A year of light ago.

The cuttings were grown
from my grandfather's garden
A galaxy away.

As for real stars,
It is said their light arrives
Long, long after their first fire dies.

The flowers on your baby blanket —
now coloured constellations
across your sweet, warm curves —
Appeared, one by one, as I sewed them,
Gladly awaiting your birth.

And so the buds are opening
As they opened before I was born

... as one eve when you are grown
you might watch the Southerly blow
and nod at the bud of a baby
and wonder how on earth ...



1994 (for my daughter, Annie)

# In suburbia

## I saw suburbia

Take me to the land of too-bright nappies! I would have said.
Fooled-right happiness!
I'll fight shabbiness
— Patches on tatters —
Everything matters.
Nobody shatters you here!

Oh, yes.
I saw suburbia
In rusty chicken wire
And dusty bricks
An annuals wilting,
Too grow-pepped to muster step support.

Well, yes.
I saw suburbia
In brave fresh eggs
And contact paper before the peel
And undies flapping,
    Red-pegged and done,
      Soaking up some sun

And an endless sigh of children
    Romping, dirty-kneed
      Uphill to tired mothers.


1980

## Housewife balad 2

Flying colours
There it ends?
Doom descends.

Anti-wrinkle creams
And backwards dreams
Of younger skin
And younger grins.

A never-ending laundry stack
More and more shopping to unpack

Where now, that wider world,
That I had dreamt of as a girl?

## Exhaustion

In the front yard, there are people trees.
Who says those ferns
Are not soft fingers
Pushing along my throat?

## Housewife ballad 3

The age of diamonds is not dead
I see it rise off my mother's head

What did the drummer, dreaming play?
What did the dreamer, scheming say?

Relax, my love, it will fade away…

Shake off the pain as you make the bed
Think of pure bright gems instead.

Times flows.
It does not step in stages
No one turns the pages of your thought.

Grey hair grows.

When did you last wonder
Where virginity goes?
Or if it ought?


1981

## Tea party

Tea set sits on a stable table.
They shift each piece in a favourite fable.

"Do you think he'll visit?"
"This china's exquisite."
"His favourite." "Is it?"
"Why did she choose it, then?"
"Does it please her to use it?" "Men!"

Tea steam rises.
They fantasise

Elude to illusions
– their fixed conclusions.

"If you knew how to get him
Do you think you would let him
Come to your arms again?"

"Nobody's eyes could melt me so.
He'd send me roses - did you know?
Oh, for his charms again!"

How it was
And how it should be…
Ladies aging,
Sipping tea.                                1981

## Housewife balad 4

The blackness turns to silver in her hands.
With eyes like crystal and head held high
She moves sans fault, without demands,
Weathering all weather as it blows on by.

The plants and children in her care, they bloom.
New leaf, new teeth - she nods, smile, knows.
Laughter is her lover. She dwells not on doom.
Principles are not her princes. Each decision grows.

Dust in the sunlight,
Cobwebs in corners,
Flour on the floor from her shisical creation
Magically blowing pain away,
Asking no return, no pay,
Turning black to silver in her hands.

Bule is blue is blue is blue, she says,
Looking at the sky
Knowing nor needing no deeper truth,
Not afraid to cry.

Sensing some design
Wondering at the shine
She turns the black to silver in her hands.

1982

## Slip out at dawn

Sometimes I think I'll leave this room.
I'll don my slippers and my gown,
Slip out, then
At the edge of town
I'll go and join the garbage men
And work all dawn with their moving tomb.

First steps on the frosty grass
Shaking all the broken glass:

That's me out there with the cold, hard steel
And I marry old tissues to orange peel.

I take heavy bins and make them hollow.
I feed excess to our roaring machine.
I wake the sleepers who only know
That it's Monday. The garbage truck has been.

1981

## Suburbia

I know that beat
Do you think they'll shock suburbia?
Crack it wide?

How can we blame them
Beating at the brick veneer

What a party!
Did you hear?
They left their litter on the fresh-mowed verge.

Now I just hide
In the softest spaces.
Warm breath of a sleeping child
At the edge of light
In dappled shade.


1998

## To their schools

Groping about in a paranoid darkness
Hoping not to offend
Not to turn you further against the possibility I might be right.

Ah, if only you would see the fiery hopes I hold
That you will open your mind
And imagine

A laughing, cooperative world
Where my children grow —
Enriched, dancing, dazzling —

In every six hours I give them to you

Day after day.


1997

## Last Day

I saw you crying, wheeling your bike
Through the school yard for the last time
Slowly, sobbing, aiming for the furthest gate.

Remember when you couldn't wait?
You'd scan the faces at the fence, for your own mum
And run to her, full of the story of the star on your collar.

And now you don't want to leave.
Here you learnt to write, and read.
And lick the sticky icing off the tuckshop fingerbuns
Scan the grass for lost coins, four-leafed clovers and lady beetles
And laugh, and trust your friends and teachers.

You've heard about high school
About drugs and study and bullies at every corner
A place where no one knows your name.

The holidays are no consolation
Can Santa bring you back your childhood?

I want to tell you life's good over here,
But you've been so happy
You can only cry.

1996

## Escape

In between, the racks of rent, rent, rent
Between those stacks of serving spoons, the plates — again, again
Between

Come shards of clarity
    Of brilliance
    Of moments in miniature, in perfect detail…

Swinging my legs on a bridge in afternoon light,
Raindrops floating from a blue sky,
Surprise in children's faces,
Snow, absolute white, bright and cold —
Warm kiss after a storm.

1996

# On focus

## A moment

Sweet camera
Capture the droplet about to drip,
Capture the lips about to sip,
Capture the fruit about to fall,
Capture the bounce of a bouncing ball.

Each will come,
As endlessly spins sea to sun
– a moment –
And it is done.

But, capture the vigil,
Sweet camera,
Or the highwire
Where anticipation and apprehension fight,
And then, sweet camera,
Will you have captured me
This night.


1977

## Still and silent

A rose is standing, still and silent
It testifies to how it looked in candlelight
And how, with me, it bathed in your gaze,
Accomplice and companion of that night.

FOND PONDER

But, now is now.
    Still and silent I sit,
    Contemplating
    Stagnating.

Conductor's baton raised and still
While silent hall sits and expects,
Full cup filled – one drip to spill,
Crest of hill on tricycle treks.

PROMISE OF POISE

    But.
Bombed concert halls?
Cracked cups?
Tricyclers called home for tea?
Poisoned poise.

And there is, too —
Still scribble script,
Fermenting lament
On a silent page.

Words, you trick me so!
It is too convenient that "yearn"
Should rhyme with "learn"
And "grow" with "know".

Inspiration all forsake,
You would govern my thought.
Through tempt of form fine wrought
You'd sway me, slay me, fake.

But come. Work with me?
Or must I tame you,
Break on through?
World view rules, not words.

You – may be my tools,
    My friends,
My fools.

We'll work as a team anon,
Or else,
Be gone!

1977

## Manipulation

Yeats – your gyre and singing schools
Rousseau – your amour propre
Eluard – the power of the poet…

Where, in this, is the me that is not me,
That pulses through my hollow fingers
Would have them tickle, cool-caress
The hearts of men and history
And how?

Oh Yeats,
You talk of Hanrahan,
All twenty years dismissed
And I, nineteen
And nineteen only now
Tick off our tryst.

Rousseau – relations externally judged
The corporate chill confusion in which I live
"I want I want" – you'd have me give
But not as the label of how I live,
Externally judged.

Eluard – poet, set my horizon!
Set my horizon to set horizons!

Here in my world.

And as the urn
As that as yet unspun
That, yet to come
When, this undone,
The thread of words wound solid to the gyre,
Holds in its strength the inch of my desire.

You and love and life confirmed,
Horizons widened wide beyond my sight
The warm and beating darkness of this night
Has set my fingers filling
Firm to learn
In singing schools
The spools my men have need and want to use.

Nineteen, and late,
Too late at night
Contrived, contrite,
I'll tear it all in hate.

But Shakespeare was young, too.
If not for him
My truths would all be new,
Horizons not all aged and dim – but true.

Fingers?
Consenting bodies understand
A gay abandon abandoned
Indulgence
Aimless bliss is harmless –
Temporary, bland.

And yet there is a power,
Deep and dangerous
That in abysmal wisdom of mind
Bids my filling fingers wait their hour.

Singing school schooled
My self might fill potential
Hollow fingers filled will play.

World – you'll hear a music beat
From out,
Beyond where sky and earth
Would seem to you
To meet.


1979 (End of Term I at Sydney Uni)

## A choice in an aeroplane

And under hip of wing
Is distance
Flat and endless deep
Insistence

Blue never yet pinching red
White cloud
Black shadow pair?

How now a neat distinction?
Through pane of glass
– just air.

Land and sky is there, no there
(finger prints on glass)

At the line we never reach.

1979

## Poetry

Structured little numbers
Born in unsuccessful slumber
Ripped parts of me –
Incurable afflictions
    Festering
    Pestered by
    "If only"s and "I wish"s and "It's not fair"s
    And "Maybe"s and "Why?"s
Insoluble.

And poetry flows,
    Flows from my riddle-rips like tears,
Soothing without solving.

1980

## Brainstorm

"Brainstorms"
"Bright sparks"
"It came to me like a flash."

Lightning in night clouds above the sea
– neurones at work

1981

## Lab rat

Tail-spun
Skull struck dumb
Life, dribbling to droplets
Trembling in transition
    These spattered brains
Of inanimate rat on a bench.

Sublimation now.
(dried blood stains)
Tis life is dispersed
    In stacks of words
        Of scientific annuals.

Graduation.
New life.
Here, the agents of reproduction
    Bend mind and paper
    Flicking the script to life in nervous flight astride
A thought.
New papers born,
(or borne in frigid flight – idle paper planes)

This dead head with its glassy eyes –
Who'll tell its unborn pea-pod babies
That it never really dies?

                                              1979

## To write or not write

And haven't I been trundled down tunnels enough,
Here, here where the traffic rumbles?
And still it roars
And I add my noise,
Trundling down tunnels.

They taught me to sing in octaves.
And every word I ever used
Was a word I'd heard
Before.
Borrowing.
Sparking echoes in pre-burrowed tunnels,
Trundling down tunnels again.

I saw the shore shining through fences.
I saw iron bars cut shadows in sun-struck misty mornings.
I saw clouds harnessed by telegraph lines,
And chocolate box scenes
Devised and divided
By the wood of window panes.

I watched an ant.
I will not commit him to the tunnel.

1979

## Driving between mirages

Driving between mirages
on a hot, flat road …
The wheels are turning
Kicking up a dust –
A static picture burning
– must –
Action suspended
Between where shimmer lingers
At the tip
Of destination's finger.

In the mirror
The gained is a vision the same.

We move in a silver frame,
Travelling between mirages
On a hot, flat road.


1980

## The blind machine of history

The blind machine of history –
Heavy, steady all-connected
– is stacking packing packages
Of mooded/panting/sweating bodies
On little scales, all un-directed
Into the slots of possibles.

And how?
They yield to their own seduction,
The dream-chasers
Drive-fast, die-young racers
Certain stepping purpose nodders, plodders
Switching, shying flights
Hero-heralded fighters …

All, all
Are moving in the gears
Patterning the years
Rolling, or rolled into roles
Of history's blind production.


1980

## Ways of seeing

"It's all a question of focus," he said,
And settled his spectacles – wise.
"See how the wound oozes, shiny in blood red?
"Come – let 'sorry' swim tears before your eyes.

"Now, look a little beyond,
"At the lavender musk
"Of yesterday's dusk
"Hazy with jasmine."

– The bruise had softened into skies.

      "See the f\*\*\*ing sunset?"
      It pokes at me between buildings and bridge stanchions,
      And I am helpless – force-fed
          Seat-belted in a bucket seat.

Livid, vivid, shameless crimson red.
–   The bandages turned purple where it bled
And it hurt. And it hurt.

Focus finds pain, too.
Seek peace and comfort?
I wonder if he knew,
That children and idlers and the curious
Can see the world through inverted glasses.        1980

# Knowledge

```
              I KNOW A STABLE TABLE OF KNOWLEDGE
                                               J
                                               E

                                               N
                                               E
I KNOW A STABLE TABLE OF KNOWLEDGE
J    S                                         J         S
E    A                                         E         A
     I                                                   I
N    S                                         N         S
E                                              E
     P                                                   P
S    A                                         S         A
A    S                                         A         S
I                                              I
S                                              S

P                                              P
A                                              A
S                                              S
```

1981

## **Illusion**

When the ice you're walking on
Breaks to space when you start to run
Then all you live might be erased
And all you give might just be waste.

If illusion is the only truth I find,
I give to you illusion of the finest kind.


1981

## Out of focus

"Ego" and "Id", they labled me,
Then subdivided time.
Monday, childhood, older, gone,
Today, tomorrow, on and on.

But maybe,
In the depth so all-surrounding
     Where glasses swallow wine from jugs
     And candle flames still stretch and shrug,
This or that is all-astounding
     Or passes un-noted in equal degree.
Maybe this judger,
     Sweeping opinion in little groups of minds,
Is tugging eddies in a tactile sea
Where water is water unconfounded
And all is wet in kind.

Maybe literature is academia's plasticine.
Who can blame a game on paper?
Minds over minds over minds
Over captured concentration over centuries
Of criticisms of criticisms of criticisms.

Is it all a question of focus?
No!
Surely awareness yields a choice!

Why accept spectacles?

We'll build some dreams beyond your fancy
With imagery beyond your glance
With any far-fetched, far-flung dance,
With tools of words (now-naked fools).
Beyond!
Beyond and further,
To daredom kingdom,

And

    Even

        Off        the                  page

1981

## Obscurity

Watching the spire bend …
Where is its shape?
It moves and warps
Thin and thick
As the rain moves down the glass

The moving hollows of me
Spaces my lost loves left …

Is it just a pane of glass
Which makes me fear
There's no solidity?


1981

## On leaving uni

Such distances!
Such libraries of books!
Stride out like a man
Shake each volume like a hand

Devour it, if you must
But do not toss and turn
There are so many things to learn.

My purpose is not to linger,
Lumbering
Nor to speak of purpose.

Seek out.
Speak out,
Of all the other things.


1982

## On working

Like a visitor
I still imagine
That I hold some other rules more dear
Liked the edges of leaves lining up
Effective
To another law
More near,
Invisible.
The ruler knows
Your systems lack some sanity
Yet I learn your salutes
Complex – a vanity
Of equivalents – blue suits
– a borrowed tie
– a borrowed sense of knowing your rules
As if some more true exist –

Oh, I waver, waver
Here in the changing,
As changing is …

No woman in man's land
Ever dwelt without a question.
Lucky us.

What of the men,
Who must adopt
Adapt with no excuses
That world
And all of its abuses? 1984

## On reporting at Federal Parliament House

Roll, rolling with the cool, smooth bark
The yards and yards of bark
Each inch unique
I'll write of children
The stuff of flesh
Cascading into the centuries

But see these men with their frowns
And strict predictions
Nod, nod, furrowed brow
The stuff of newsprint

Cold cafe bar coffee
Tepid convenient friendships forgotten
Bereft of even the burn of ice
As they make noise at the next new desk.

Oh, I could tell you of cool, pre-dawn clouds,
Another ether
Soothing as holiday sunburn cream, cool
Nestling at the foot of the hills
Soft, soft.

Alarms. Firm feet down the corridors
And firmer faces,
The seriousness etches into sweat

Which cannot flow like the workers'
In grateful beads
Gravity led, honest.
But is mopped before the cameras catch the shine
And washed and erased daily from your suits

But I know you know of nights
When the lid of the sky is open

This seriousness is such a business
And our business is to listen
And chase.

While,

With nothing but the chink of dawn birds
Snatched cups of tea before the desk's force orders us
Spoons on china
As the steam rises
With smooth, cool bark.
The gums still grow.

1985

# Journalist 2

I drink ink
Black in, that slinks, thick, into the bowels of our building,
Liquid cylinder

I tap out patterns
Spatters on paper
Mundane muse
The daily news

On the third floor,
The message is magnified
Mirriored images slapped and slapped
And stacked and trucked

There, blown against fences,
Old papers
Telling of our capers
Of politics and power
Of pop stars and racers,
The rumours, the defences
In past and present tenses
TV guides and horoscopes
News of peasants news of popes

Black link on link
The thread of ink.

I drink ink
Printed on the packet
My name, my claim, my pay,
For bed, for food, for drink
For using up the ink.

1985 (at *The Sydney Morning Herald*)

## Rejecting journalism

Give fact the flick
In favour of fiction
The flavour of friction's
A hateful affliction.

"Expert slams sham"

"Hurt hit scandal"

Go and label another alarm.
Oh, give me calm!

Somewhere, words slumber
Drifting in limbo
Humble buttons without holes.


1986

# Of love and longing

## First kiss?

I knocked at your door
And called your name.
I knocked again,
But no one came.
You said you'd be here
But clearly you're not
Perhaps you don't care.
Perhaps you forgot.
I wish you'd come
I want you so
You seemed so Nice
But now I know
That how you live
Is all take, not give.
It wasn't for this
That I gave you a kiss.

1972

## Before the concert

The lights dim
Yes, madam,
I feel its weight and warmth –
Prize pelts, expensive gift –
To someone special
For far, far more
Than the instant
Of the gentleman's wink for me
As I gained my seat.

The curtain rises
You whisper to your husband
And as you turn
Your fur coat bares my skin.
It leaves it cold
Where your nonchalant toss had brushed it covered
To warm – and to warn.
Yes, madam.
I respect your property.


1976

## Be with me

Wide is the valid tally of faces
Of books and films and trendy places
Wide races time, saves it dancing
Scoring quick kisses, skimming, glancing.

But pause.
Stare into me,
And dare me.

Be with me,
Deeper than the wide.


1979

## One

The bones of the paddock
Were clenched fists
The clouds were islands
– too far away.

"Lost-along-the-way-lost along …"
    Spat at me
In grey computer lists

But you have held and been with me,
calm in warm skin warmth.
And you have polished me
To a smooth marble shine in your palm.

Kick-drops of sea in sun.
You scattered me
In liquid, living marbles
Laughing.
One.


1979

## **Break up**

With you there is nothing to fight for
With you there is nothing to share
Any anyone's fingers are welcome
To slip like the breeze through my hair.

You know you won't hold me tonight for
Tomorrow we'll be who knows where.
So why should your face and your words come
To mean more than trees passing there?

A horse is standing in shadow
A bicycler rides on a line
Position and time and possession?
A windmill just turns in sunshine.

When empty blows cold through the darkness
When stones are grown hard to my touch
When nothing is near to be with me
I wonder if I'll miss you much.

1979

## Candle Hands II

And I will call you freedom,
And prosperity
And peace
And hold you to me;
Hold you, holding me.

And you, you're in the candle flame:
I lean against the light.
And pure and slow you warm me through,
'cause fire
Never dies.

Mid thunder in the winter chill
And mad demands a-knocking at my door,
Warm and calm
in the curve of your arm
I melt.

And flesh and bones
Are soft and strong
And what you own
Is somewhere you belong.

So hold me to you;
Hold me, holding you.
The mold is true.
Let me lean against the flame.               1981

## Words in the bed with bodies

Arc of nose
Cove of arm
And out
There,
Where you move without me

Stark of clothes
Palm to palm
Pout
Stare
Bare, you tumble about me.

Dark it chose
Blows warm
Shout
Scared
Snared, you dove within me

Fudges
Breath blown Frozen
Shrug

Toes, not prose.
With wordy charm
We doubt
"Care?"

"Share?"
"You humbly win me?"

Unknown oceans
And lone emotions
Are words in the bed with bodies
Rhyming notions.

While arc of nose
And cove of arm
Sleep.


1982

## More words

Harlequin men
And dusky eye access,
Practice poutings
Smoother success.

Well, there are too,
The slow and sober slaps
Of great Aunt's brooch
Shooting diamantes
Out of a headland –
Streetlights through a sea mist
At me.

But the knowing
And the wondering
That surfaces with champagne –
Excludes
Till wide and shiny
Sits the old distinction
Of where I am
And where I'd wish to be

But this remains –
The words I write
For no man's jelly bean rewards.
These words I choose.
And these are my final joys, today:

Gum trunks clutching
A dying sky
Gold with slap-dash
Day-old sun.

And all the people
Talk about themselves,
Including me –
See?


1982

## If I could know

If I could know
That when I felt your charm
You were just charming me,

If I could know
That when we laughed,
You were just humouring me

If I could know,
That when you found me in the dark
You were just bending,
     Condescending,
Vending me magic, a memory

Then I would know to be upset,
Leave in regret,
grieve

Then could I grow, to forget.


1981

## Seeking love

As in youth
When dreams of warmth and touch
Sustained me
So now in dreams
Past loves and lusts
Return.
The jewelled dresses
Stained and faded
As I knew they must
And memories fester.
I guessed then I'd yearn.
How could I hold you tight enough
to hold back time?

1990

## That privileged life

We glimpsed that life
That glorious life
Of privilege and importance
Itineraries and famous names,
Ah yes.

And yet
Who now, as you are tired and old and hot
In the wide and insect laden dusk …
Who will watch the sun dip with you
As you sit on the garden bench,
alone?


1992

## Returning to Women's College after 19 years

I hear the bells,
And I am there again.
I am every young woman in a black robe
I am every parent, beaming
And every pomped academic – awkward – something more than skin and bones
Yet something less than stone.

I climb the steps
And am there again.
Dark wood encloses me
And I remember – privilege and ignorance – Ms Miss or Mrs,
a self-importance that has never gone away,
Wanting only to give and love.
So tentative.
Impotence, influence, and enough big words to sink a ship, or sail away.

I remember hunger, confusion, expectations never met,
And yet,

Was I the fruit that dropped and rotted?
What worthwhile seeds have I spread?
I hear the bells

And in the garden of my soul
You are all my summers.

2001 (for Bruce)

## Circles of nine

Deep in the forbidden flatlands
Are circles of nine,
Prayers in stone
Portent of power
A link with the gods.

At the tourists' shop
I buy my trinkets
Nine tiny circles of stone
To share with friends.

As if we can be linked,
As if with gifts they will accept my need for them.

In the park
The rush, rush, rush of wings,
Reminds me of the order.

A desperate bird offers up its throat,
And may be spared.


2008

# On flora and fauna

## Westerly Wind

Blown down by the wind on a cold autumn night
Westerly westerly westerly wind
Just a bunch of feathers and two eyes, bright
Westerly westerly wind

He lay on the ground with his little head tilted
Westerly westerly westerly wind
Like a tiny grey flower with its petals wilted
Westerly westerly wind

So sad he looked, so cold and lonely
Westerly westerly westerly wind
That I picked him up when I saw him below me
Westerly westerly wind.

1970

## Mistletoe

Welcome.
Deliciously garnish my smooth, young flesh
With your strange and delicate darkness.

Excite my innocence as you cling
And pierce deeper,
Deeper within me,
Relentlessly

Thrill.
Pain.
Panic.

You drink from my own life core.
Strangling,
I struggle in silence,
Hopelessly.

My soul devoured,
What remains for you to steal and suck
But dismal, shattered scars,
Strange and delicate
As mistletoe leaves?


1975

## Frangipani

Frangipani magic
Swimming the distance
Slicking the dust with light
Mundanity's gladness.

Skimming existence
Dust on mighty pistons.
Midges in the night
Frangipani madness.

1979

## Honeysuckle

As with honeysuckle,
Heavy with the hum of bees,
This air is thick with songs unsung
And thoughts at the tip of the tongue
Sweetness hangs in the air.

1979

## Pippies

Slow
 Pippies edging into sand.
  Sly.

     Flow
      Cloud dispersing into sky
      Fly.

          Blow
           Wind edging into instants
             Nimbus shifting into distance

No
   Clouds just     blow
                                            away

1981

## Silver moth

Silver moth –
Calling down the hollows where it flew
Powder dust
Powder dust
–   Is drowning in the mist

It left its edge on every flight it made.

So this is age –
All the layers gone –
Silver, lost and drifting in the mist.

The silver dust is lifting.
The silver moth
Calls.



1981

# Chernobyl

Most powerful poison
Will hurt the world
And then return.

In what new sadnesses
Will it show itself
Seeping down the seasons?

And this new law we made
We will obey
Having, as we will
to live its verdict
Crippled, in ever new ways.

And once familiar,
Will we stop to look for reasons?
That first news shook our senses.
And seeing ourselves defenceless
We could but choose
To half ignore
Our new ghost
Growing, as we will
To learn to live with it.

1985

## Jewels

I am not old
I can still see the harbour
As black velvet in the night
And the Opera House,
familiar shape
Still shows new beauty.

Off with my high heels!
Barefoot on the turf
I bounce.

Because…
Didn't you see the green grass
Growing in cracks
In the median strip
While cars flashed past
Coating them with fumes?

Covered in dust, they grow,
Such filthy, precious jewels!


1985

## Gum trunks in spring

Darkness drops.
New copper blooms.

In spring,
In soft purple greys
the bark of the red gums
breaks and falls.

In the new year,
Orange and pinks,
jigsaw shapes.
'til whole trunks are smooth and new,

Last year's bark spreads out along the ground
and hangs in bracken,
sheltering lizards

All the crackling pages of last year's stories.


1986

## Heavy, heavy rose

Heavy, heavy rose
The petal cups of scent
Are soft palms,
     Asking,
So vulnerable,
I'd swear the scent were solid
–  Aromatic amber
Some dust of preciousness
Powder, powder soft
–  Oh smell these cups of blush.


1986

## These trees

These trees
Whose roots reach deeper
Than the veins in your hand
For longer than your life, strong man

Whose bodies hardly shudder
Under the muscles of your arm, strong man
Whose leaves drink secrets from the air you breathe
And shimmer, shimmer

And so you run to your teeth of steel,
Strong man
And with the stink of strength
You stole from ancient woods
You meet again
These trees.

Only that crack, that ache of torn timber
Can talk, if you will hear
Of bright lorikeets, lost
And possums, searching, searching for favourite perches,
Gumnuts gone.

Now rest,
Strong man, in the midday heat
But do not ask for shade.
Those trees.
Time will grey their broken limbs
As it will fell you, too, strong man.     1988

## Fishermans Parade

Can roots break rocks?

Deep in damp
the chrysalis stirs.

Can roots break rocks?
So soft and slow
the minute cilia grow.

Can roots break rocks?

Shrugging off dust
So they emerge.

Cicadas rise

On wings compelling

To cling to the canopy
and sing…

And roots break rocks.

1990

## Bogong moths

Bogong moths
Beneath my house
Beside the sea
Are dark shapes in the cool dawn
A feather-soft and fluttering mosaic –

Bogong moths
Down from the mountains

Once summer's treat.
What memory makes me reach to touch, in wonder?

Ah, to hold these ancient shapes,
And make the feast!
But who can show me how?

My hands grasp emptiness, clumsy,
As dark shapes dissipate.


1993

## Gardenia

Gardenia
Cool and smooth as my mother's cheek
Kind and fresh as my mother's voice,
All these years

Let me worship these twin blessings –
A mother whose love still nurtures me
And this flower
– white beacon in the dusky darkness.

They feed my soul.


2017 (for my mother)

## This black bean seed

This black bean seed
Is comfort in my hand,
As I smooth and turn it,
Smooth and turn it,
Knowing you will go.

And in my mind,
It turns in the dark Sydney soil,
Sends down its root
Sends up its trunk
Lets loose its leaves
One by one
To link across the southern sky
And shelter me
From space, so infinitely cold.

The Great Hall stands
And the organ lends a glory
To this pain of parting.

Another crop of graduands
And one of them is mine.
Third generation to rise
and doff,
and walk away.

As I am soothed
by the promise of other lives to come

And this seed.


2010

(Upon Casey's graduation and decision to do his Phd at Caltech, USA)

# On time and place

## In the Great Hall

The Great Hall is of
Rock-solid neutrality, old,
Rigid-distanced-set-square walls,
Gravity-flat floor
And stone certainty

    Time is predictable
Tick of clock
Century after century.

Lovely, spinning, dizzy dance
Mingling, tingling, living jives
Movement-mix of laughter, lives,
We spin and grin in liquid glance.

    A stone gargoyle grimaces.
Time is predictable.
Glances at dances
Generation after generation.

But look!
The straight-cut steps are worn to curves!

Time is risky
As the sweat slippery grip
Of spin-linked fingers

Solid and alive.                    1979

## The tempo infinite

They put the record by the fire
And laughed to think of music melting
I watched a guitar slowly die
As the man unwound its strings

But
By the sea, I saw the world spin into night
And felt the tempo infinite.


1979

## McMahons Point

While too-slim people eat their deprivation
Angling down pavements, with interesting eyes
The bridge is licking the last of the sun
And in that last mouthful
A pinked yacht sails beneath
And I am thinking –
Freedom binds,
But slavery blinds
And Aku Raku is up for sale.

I see you in pay, flexing your biceps,
Aku Raku tugging at the mooring
Sinking into the red in a bank's balance files –
Windowed envelopes drop into letterboxes …

The night lights are on around the harbour
And I think of other things.

Next morning's sun feeds the opposite view.
I must be satisfied with balance,
If not with boats.

Pastel sky sits behind the champagne cork
Which dresses our balcony.
Both hide behind the mist
The kettle gave the glass;
– but I must go to work.

1982

## Kirribilli

It is real glitter
It is true glitter
This is twilight bounced off every ripple
Ever-changing facets of harbour
     Bounce it up at me.

Details of twilight – impressions stake a claim.

Do not tell the landlady.

Imagination wraps itself around a dot.
She'll have us paying double for our lot.


1984

# Sydney Harbour

Some smooth words, smooth as still night on the harbour,
Lapping black, hushed oily palms, empty,
Holding the down-draft of night,
Heavy, heavy dew.

Some bright words, frisky as light on the harbour,
Spattering, breezy, against the edges,
Tweaking at the opera wall
Sucking at the wharf support
Water sports
In the morning, new.

Dull flat pewter.
Neuter.
Colourless and lank,
The harbour's wet blanket
Is the carpet in a rented flat,
Used.

With its wet and weighty eye
The harbour looks up at the sky
Sees buildings, boats and people change,
Summing up Sydney in all its moods.

Puff, puff, magic breath
Under our bridge,
Where the harbour blinks ...
Steel lashes stirring up the breeze.

1984

# Glendower Avenue 3am summers

I do
I miss the ciacadas
The hot, humid Christmas crush
Of insect wings on insect limbs
Rasping out into dawn
And on
Just past the heavy dusk
Cicada
Cicada

The buzzy, hanging air
- Dark as the tacky, sweaty, party sparkle stars
Are bright…
Gardenias and peaches,
And the old gold of Christmas beetles
Bashing their age-old shapes
Against the night light.

Bare feet
On still warm steps,
Strappy sandals hanging in one hand
Like the deliciousness
Of summer-hot skin
Still burning from days on sand.

These were the days
That were the longest,
The most alive,
The holiday blessed best
Stretching to

Later than late returns
And happy awakenings
As again
The first cicada sings.


1986

## Half Tide Rocks

The tide is running
Fast flowing water
Kourong Gourong
Past Half Tide Rocks

The wind is singing
All through the rigging
Moonee Moonee
Spirits in the wind

The bellbirds are calling
It's timber they're hauling
The tide is falling
Past Half Tide Rocks

The birds are going
Now traffic is flowing
And Coorumbine's dry
Past Kendall's rock.

The sands are shifting
Half Tide Drifting
Profit and loss
Past Half Tide Rocks

Do you ache for a breeze
For the breath of the trees?
Have you seen the bush burning
Past Half Tide Rocks?

I've seen you in flood
With the land weeping mud
And the debris churning
Past Half Tide Rocks

And Judibarn
Are you my heart?
The waves are breaking
Past Half Tide Rocks

Adrift, adrift
Moonee and mourning
Awaiting high tide
And a Kincoimba dawning

The children are yearning
For dolphins returning
Is the tide turning
Past Half Tide Rocks?

We may nurture old seed
In this wasteland of greed
We may learn the old words
From the call of the birds

The tide is running
Fast flowing water
Kourong Gourong
Past Half Tide Rocks

1994

# Nielsen Park

You can meet yourself at Nielsen Park
Where the wash of waves
Comes calm, calm
Calm as you knew in your mother's womb
Calm as her sleeping breath.

You can meet yourself at Nielsen Park
Wince-bright waves, liquid glitter…
You can meet yourself there
Salt in the air
Every rasp of sand, a memory
Every ice cream sweet against salt,
City at your back.

Enter the brine,
And you are every baby, child and lover
Every aging body, held
Suspended in the elements
Of sea and sky and sun.


2001

## North Coast Nights

North coast nights.
Mild.
One long, hot beach,
Mile upon mile.
More stars than you've ever seen.
Places you belong,
Calling you back…

The rich volcanic earth
Bananas, the cane, the weeds
Can anything really grow that fast?

No wonder then, they've found the place,
Developers buying up sea views
And peddling them (farewell good cows)
For prices people only pay
When buying back their youth.

North coast nights
Sweet rasp of sand on sunburnt skin
Salty swigs of clean sea mist
One lungful after another
Mother, lover, sister, brother
You've been here before.

One long hot summer?
All your summers back again,
Held in gentle air
With frogs and crickets and the long lap of waves to shore.
You've been happy here before.

What pleasures then are yet in store
Here on north coast nights?


2001

## Berrys Bay dusk

The winter dusk
Is pastel musk
Is shimmering pink
Off Berry's Bay

The musk sticks rise
On the city horizon
Past the darkening park
Of misty grey.

2001

## Green Cape Escape

White gate to space
Witness the heaving sea
See where the wind's salty fingers
Have woven a rocky filigree

White gate to space
To an endless ceiling of stars
To a seabed embroidered with wondrous weed
Look up to see Saturn and Mars

White gate to space
To an endless parade of clouds
The white, the grey, the pink and the peach
With the salt and the sun, to clean and to bleach
And the wind and the waves
In the heath and the caves
And the sea, and the sea, and the beach…

You see…
White gate to space

What bracing isolation
What wealth of distance
Of privacy and peace

This place.
Green Cape. Escape.                    2004

# Under the moon and sun

## Build me a backwash

Sick, sick, sick of proving
That I have nothing to prove to anything
Sick, sick, sick of analysing
Analysis.

Oh – build me a backwash of some nameless
      nothing
        place

And bury me in paralysing
dynamism,
with an audience of absent non-existence.


Or –
Wind – spin me a web
and sling me, slung, in its bed of neglect.

Then I'll reflect,
      burying my head in forgotten dreams
and temptings so empty
that even regret

isn't.


1974

## Under the moon

A moonbeam drips from my fingertips
Touchable light
Dependable night
Stars, and cool, hard moonbeam light
Shadows dark – ink-dappled
Outline stark – silver-tipped

Honest moon staring
Intensity scaring

Sobering

Steadying

Still.


1976

## Zephyr caresses

Zephyr caresses
Of white silk dresses
On Sunday afternoons

Be-ribboned bonnets
Shakespeare's sonnets
Twine-tamed balloons

Gentlemen reading
Children duck-feeding
Duck waddling makes them wonder

Ladies promenade
Under parasol shade
Notes float from under rotunda.

1976

## Sky-blue balloons

Sky-blue balloons with velvet ribbons
Fresh and new and shy,
Tentatively touching
Bumping with the breeze
Floated, soaring, way up high
Up, up above the clouds
Shared the view
Swelled with joy
And broke …

On the ground
Magic shattered
Clumsy rubber, scattered

And somewhere,
Velvet ribbons.

1976

## **Seasons**

Come, Lucifer, and we'll defy the dandelion queen
And slip like fingers through ripe corn tassels.

Oh hold me
Hold me
Mold me golden

For I am the warmth of sunny-side cherries
Come tumble, dazed, the humming heat haze
and slide the shine on summer berries

Yes, Lucifer, but come,

For well we know that your thunderstorm arbour
Yawns and stretches and dreams of drifting

And well we know that the seeds I harbour
Must have their chance at tomorrow.

Summer will slash us wide
And let
    them
        fall.


1978

## Into the wind

Into the wind, my friend
Into the soft slow bend
Into the curve all sadly smooth
Still or flowing you're bound to move.

Into the edge of a bar of sun
Into the cloud-clotted sky
Elliptical blue
Swallows you

Hail the flailing curtain on its rail
– a friend in the business existence entails
We hide in rooms
But still it consumes

– This movement blend.

We are sent or
Taken
Into the wind or
By it,

Moving

1980

## Still things

Still things.
Shhh.
We will go quietly,
Like locusts in the fall.
We all make mistakes.

Slow
Behind the iris of an eye –
Something clear

Sunlight
Spilt and settled on the floor
The window let it loose

Reprimanded now.
The window's blinded
But grins.
The floor is warm.

Whisper drift
Marble cool on pulsing wound
Soft wind.
Tapered minutes, out of the images
– the things on which your history sits

Into

Soft – into waves

Lapping into peace.                                   1980

## Under the moon and sun

Wind – through the night vine
Yes, dance, my droplets as you sine
This rain dance
– spirit through the body
These tears and this delight …

God, surely you are a great wind
Rustling the leaves,
Making our shell bodies dance –

We chatter, bump and crumble
In fashions of talk and dress
– this season's rain.

1981

## **A gust**

It's just the
      Just the atmosphere having a stretch
A tongue that now knows
What it's looking for.
A well-used broom
Across the floor
An unassuming zephyr
Nosing out along the lake
Rustling up texture
      Like sandpaper
      Rasping at the eye
Raking off light
Some sparkle dust
And nothing more.

Wind …
      Blows.

1986

## Autumn afternoon

There are hours
Of warmth all around
A holdingness of knowing whole-ness

The heart and limbs and mind alive
    And humming.

This is of a tiredness
That does not ache

But rests like a thing suspended
Between sky and earth

On a frail and fragrant edge
Of grass on a river bank
In an autumn afternoon.


1986

## Country women

You can see the town in its women
Pancake on crow's feet
Perfect plastic pearls around sun spotted throats
And pantihose, never mind the heat.

Self-sacrificing women
Sweating in the heat
Making their way through the paved grid
Past the parks where no-one plays
Because forefathers never raised childing
Past the wilting pansies, too bright for the drought
Along the bare banks of the flaccid river
Aching for shade
And the sun twists the knife, flashing off chrome
As the cars and trucks roar

But the wives wince and bear it.
Progress? Just getting along, been better…

Remember, barefoot on the soft earth
Breathing cool, green life?
Dappled laughter, sweet creeks?

Come now, country women.
Can't you cry out, for more?


1992

## Watching waterfalls

Straddle a hot rock
Draw down the sun
Deep into your bones
And consider these cascades

Study the slick, sliding city of drips
And lose all your troubles
In the tumbling of bubbles.

No symphony
No carving in stone
No poem
Can capture this,
This glimpse of glory.

Every ache dissipates
Every regret, every last lingering fear
Is lost, lost and ever falling
Down where the smashed water drifts,
Where ozone lifts.

No symphony
No carving in stone
No poem
Can capture this,
This whispering of infinity…

1999

## Waterfalls

Waterfalls
Simply
Under the law of gravity
Tumble

A leaf
Reaches its green palm out
To the sun

And I am drinking in the wind

Slow and steady
Turns the world
The planets stare

While I sleep.


2001

## Five bells

Five bells?
Five boats, times five, times five

And she is queen of the beach
She is, she is,
Say the waves
She is queen of the beach

Five bells?
Five boats – those floating facets
Five sails, times five, times five
So very much alive

More dignity than I can muster
Sand in the eyes in a Southerly buster
Queen of the beach.


2001 (For the smiling, suntanned octogenarian at Nielsen Park)

## Sun

All day it plays
Dappled through my garden
These discs of bright
These slices of light
A showering of golden coins
Myriad riches
This summer sun.


2004

## I own the sun

I own the sun
I own the sky
So don't come at me with your cracked Humpty Dumpty shell in shards
Your breaking heart
The grief.
"Gonna die
"Better say goodbye."
No.

I own the yolk
So whole and golden
And I am rich.

I own the earth
The smell of rain
And tears like ice
With the wind on my cheeks
My heart is warm and full
And beating.
Feeling.

I own the sun.

2022

## A writing corner in Sierra Madre

Hear the river
In this canyon corner
Washing away – forever.

It draws forth words
And better words,
Of tales to share.
Shh.
Hear the river.

Birds lace distance
With wings and calls.
Mist lifts.

Hear the river.
Slowly, sun washes the valley,
Gold.

A thousand brassy trumpets blare.

No.
Sun blazes.

2023

# Of grief and gratitude

## Age

Ah now
That your skin –
Soft warm curves –
Is grey and heavy,
Muscles shrinking
Hanging on your bones
Like a rolled up sail

Now that you lie,
"so tired"
And only your mind
In that dome
Still smooth and full between the temples
Is lively,

You are closing your eyes
Jumping back and forth
Between the decades
As you clambered up mossy gullies
And strode down beaches

With your racing axe
You split the years.
Chips fly –
Places,
Faces
Gone but not forgotten,
Yet,
while your chest rises again.

Even your words are falling away
Is it hard to talk,
Lying down, listener in tears?

Stories
And favourite places
You will leave for us
"Yes"
And my own slackening skin and tiring bones
One quarter yours…

Almost gone
Golden light
End of the wick
When the candle flame blows out.

Sheet lightning
Plays in the temples of cumulonimbus.
Never reaching Earth,
It drifts away.

As the bushfire –
Tangerine smudge on the night horizon –
Expunges spring's intricate flowers
With its hot breath

As the sun
Slips behind the ridge
Striking glitter from cold, hard hail.

I think of you, under the ground
Your stubble would glint like cut straw
And you would marvel that it grows.


1993 (for Hector)

## Brave Heart

When I look down and see my hands
I see your hands – fine-tuned machines.
Five thousand lives or so you saved,
Dancing the needle through deepest flesh,
Mending the saddest secrets of our hearts.

Look closely now at "skill"
So close a word to "kill"
They cannot think you won't be missed.
My fingers tighten to a fist.

They barely said goodbye to you
When you put down the knife.
No "thank you" for the time you gave,
The extra hours and nights and years,
Stolen from your life.

We say courage is a quality
Whose centre is the heart.
So while it beats we dry our tears.

Look up.
Fresh start.
Give a wave
Brave heart.


1997 (for Tim, at his retirement from NSW Health)

## Unfinished

Confronting the dregs of our dreams
So little to show
For a lifetime of laughter?

Tell me, when moonlight dapples in
Over the chips of our chopping block
That all the wood we burned
Still warms us

Why are the dreams so simple
And so whole?
Why is the reaching so fragmented?
So many interruptions
So much waste.

1999

# Theft

There among the trousers of Slessor's
I saw them all,
The misplaced shells of other people's lives.

It wasn't that they stole my jewels,
Those literal links
Those gifts once given
The hands that gave
Those faces, places,
The smooth-skinned girl that once I was
The smell of spring – not lost, not lost

It wasn't that they bulldozed my grandparents' house
Such solid sandstone foundations
Such secure proportions,
–   Still it stands, in my mind.

The petals fall
But the space remains,
That vivid shape that they defined
That fine idea of a flower,
So beautifully fulfilled…

Or so I say.
It wasn't that they took my flute away.
The skill remains, or so I say.
My memories, my memories,
Comforting incantation in a world of change.
Disquiet stilled.

2000

## When I am dead

Somewhere, between the singing and the song
Between the giving and the gift
Between the living and the life
Between the striving and the strife
Between the touching and the touch
Between the bleeding and the blood
Between the choosing and the choice
Between the verses and the voice
Between the thinking and the thought
Between the buying and the bought
The teaching and the taught
The catching and the caught
Breathing and breath
Beating and beat
I was.
You are.

2004

(At 17, Casey joked I should call this
"Between the coughing and the coffin"!)

## **Pneumonia**

In the labyrinth of my mind
Through the darkest depths I wind
Caught in tunnels of dark despair
Where I grope for comfort and gasp for air

Round and round I writhe and turn
Where I cry and worry and fret and yearn
Where the past is lost – I can no longer go
And the pressing fear is all I know

Fear of tomorrow, what I cannot see
Where my hands are tied, and I cannot be
Where is the person who used to be me?
Caught in this labyrinth – I long to be free.


2005

## For Hector

You are every old man
In a hat and flannelette shirt
Sleeves rolled up.

And I am you –
Sniffing the fresh breeze
Lapping up the dappled warmth
      Of a north coast sun

Grinning at the nippers' birthday party in the park

As the baby's soft hair
Catches the light and shines

This glorious day.


2016

## Family

Who could have known
Our sky would crack
That this elliptic
Would start to bend and roar
And spin and split asunder?

This family orbit.

May you hold hands and heal.

For who is there to notice
the crack widen

When we spin off and are gone?


2018

## Dance of the discs

Jingling, tingling coins
All up and down my spine, but
This is the time for the stately dance,
The most beautiful ballgown of all
The straps of sinews,
The growth of angel wings
Beneath crepe skin
Holding my head high
To dance all day,
And in the evening,
To let my discs hover
and shimmer like fireflies
In descending dark
Laughing against gravity.
Up and up again, up
Defying death's
final cascade.

2012

## Take me at high tide

Take me at high tide
In among the mangroves
Where mud coloured fish
Nubble at the fuzzy seabed.

They feast on fallen bees,
Busy wings too worn for flight.

Down, softly down,
We are all drawn,
'til the world is just one backwater
One quiet cove,
So still, there is just
A glistening reflection
Of the glorious trees and sky.

We are released.

Take me at high tide.


(for Roslyn)

## Butterflying

You looked so light when you lay down.
Light of bones
And light of heart

Did you feel too heavy
To rise again?

I hope your mind was light
And free to fly and flutter
To somersaults in the playground
Warm eggs in winter pockets
And then
To serving the nation.
Dash dit, dash dash dash, dit dash dit, dash dash, dit dash

Be free, be free!
Free to touch on past loves, and your beloved babies
To all those parties
To all the gowns your fingers made
To every flower you painted and admired.

"Happy landings," you said to me,
before my own flight – an earthly one – in a tin can.
I wish I'd said the same to you.
But how could I voice my last goodbye?

God be with you, Butterfly.

    2020 (For Norma, with thanks to Elena Kats-Chernin)

# Celebration

I loved the sound of water,
Of the rush of foam along the shore, the hiss
As each tiny bubble burst,
Returning to sea and sky.

I loved the sound of leaves
Their frisson in a quickening wind,
That busy bustle as they brushed and slapped each other
Like the rubbing of eager hands together, skin sweeping skin, air kisses
Or dry leaves, scattering, sweeping the street.

I loved the sound of the highest notes
Piccolo, xylophone, sopranino recorder
Highest trumpet through tightest lips
Swish of brush on snare…

And yet.
Resist, stress, protest or jest.
I can't pretend.

This concert was always going to end.


2020

## Kite at a beach

Perfect shade and breeze —
Colourful kite in a blue, blue sky

Golden sand
White foam on the waves —
Between the headlands, a wide horizon.

*Mercurial sea*

*Rips hide.*
Sandbars drift and sink.

The kite dives.
In my stomach,
*Kite like a knife.*

Ah kite,
Take my soul higher.
Let me farewell my beautiful friend with grace,
Grateful for our time together.

Soar up, tiny kite, beyond this pain.

For what is grief but gratitude
For everything we shared.


2024 (for Karen)

## In the dark garden

In the dark garden – la tristesse.
Fallibility.
Fractures
Loss – slow, yet irrevocable.

Let us tiptoe through the dark garden.

Let us find white flowers,
As tendrils reach for the sun.


2024

## Always

Before the world wide web
And publishing platforms
And #metoo and social media

Before mobile phones
And rocket ships
And television

There was
My need

Your shoulder
Your hug
Your hand

Your smile
Your joy
Your wonder

And my smile
My joy
My wonder

And now?
– Still –
Beyond words and always.
My gratitude.

2024 (for my mother)

## I will come to you

I will come to you in the dawn light,
and when the mist is lifting.

I will come to you at midday,
when the sun rolls about the canyon,
— centre of my flower,
and wash you with light.

I'll tell of all the times I held you and we laughed.

At dusk and deep in the dark,
I will come to you in memories
When you call.

## About the Publisher

Lorikeet Press publishes feel-good fiction for readers of all ages. If you enjoy books with uplifting endings, you're in the right place.

Visit www.lorikeetpress.com for more information.

www.ingramcontent.com/pod-product-compliance
Lightning Source LLC
Chambersburg PA
CBHW031252290426
44109CB00012B/552